Guidebook To Setting Up A Family Trust

Jeffrey Mackie

CONTENTS

PROLOGUE

In the time that I have been preparing this book, Alberta's tax rate on the so-called '1%' of top income earners has increased from 10% to 15% at the top level. Combining this with the tax rate increases that are proposed in the upcoming federal budget on top income, moving the top tax rate from 29% to 33%, the new marginal tax rate in Alberta for 2016 will be 48% for individuals making more than $300,000 per year. This is up from 39% and represents an increase of 23% in the last 12 months on the top income earners in the province. While it isn't quite as high as what the top income earners pay in some other provinces like Ontario or Quebec, it is a massive jump in a very short period of time.

These rate increases assume that in Alberta, the NDP's budget will pass and at the federal level the Liberal party's proposed tax increase will also make it into the federal budget and take effect in 2016. With the NDP currently holding 80 of 89 seats in the Alberta legislature I think that they will manage to slide this vote through. At the federal level the representation in the House of Commons isn't quite so one-sided, but given the majority government in power it is also a safe bet that taxes will be going up across Canada.

This book will outline a compelling tax saving strategy that high income earning families should be using to structure their investments. Even at the prior tax rates, setting up a Family

Trust was a compelling tax saving strategy. With even higher taxes coming this year, the potential tax savings are even greater and the impetus is even stronger to set one up as soon as possible. The other timely factor that I will explain is that it is a great way to take advantage of the current low interest rate environment for funding the trust. Interest rates are at all-time lows and this makes funding the trust even more efficient at the moment.

The goal of this book is to simplify the concept and educate in layman's terms on what a Family Trust is, how they work and how you could use one as part of your investment strategy to save taxes and protect your wealth. Trusts are a simple structure, but are one of the most useful tools available for income splitting, protecting assets and saving taxes.

INTRODUCTION

I have had a good deal of first-hand experience with Family Trusts in my line of work, but I will admit that I definitely procrastinated in setting one up for my own family. I originally heard of the concept of a Family Trust from a friend that had one setup on his own. He explained the structure as a unique tax saving plan for a family with children. We both have similar sized families with children who attend the same school, and have a similar roster of after school extracurricular activities and associated expenses. I looked into how a trust works and knew that I had saved up enough investable assets and also have the family situation where it made a lot of financial sense to set one up.

I could have setup a Family Trust much sooner, but I only acted on it when I had all three of my children in private school. I am not sure why I waited so long when it would have made just as much sense to get started when the first one or even the second child were in kindergarten. As I'm sure any parent with young children knows, life is always busy and there is always something that demands your attention, so I don't fault anyone for not being on top of every detail of their financial picture or an expert on the latest developments that the CRA has dreamed up for changes to the Income Tax Act. This is why you hire your advisors, but they can only start setting things up when you ask them to. The responsibility is still on individuals to take the first step.

Doing the math after the fact, I probably could have saved myself roughly $10,000 per year in taxes over a couple of years by acting sooner. I think it was just the natural tendency to procrastinate on doing something that you know is good for you in the long run, but feels like a bit of a nuisance or seems difficult in the short term. The other issue is that you never see the money until tax time once per year in April, and even then it is hard to quantify the direct savings, as you don't actually see the cash leaving your bank account and going to the government every single month. One strong incentive is that once the trust is setup, funded, and invested you will actually see money going into your bank account each month to pay for things you are already paying for anyway. I have seen it firsthand, and it is a pretty good feeling seeing the cash come in when you need it.

I have gone through the process of setting up and managing my own Family Trust for a number of years now and I am seeing the ongoing benefits. I could have saved quite a bit of money by acting sooner and I won't ever get those tax dollars back. Hopefully, by reading this short guidebook you can learn if a Family Trust makes sense for you. If it does, there is no reason to wait to set one up.

The main criteria for whether setting up a Family Trust makes sense for your situation are:
-are you a high-income earner?
-do you have investments or cash saved up and already invested outside of an RRSP? or in a corporation?
-do you have people in your family at lower income levels? (elderly parents, children, spouse etc?)

If you answered yes to these questions, then you would most likely benefit from this great strategy - Let's get started!

An introduction to the Family Trust - What is it, and is it right for me?

The Family Trust is an old, tried-and-true system. Historically, the concept of the 'Trust' goes back to British common law, dating back hundreds of years ago. It is based on a strong foundation for families to build family-oriented wealth and assets, setting up deep roots and passing assets or property from generation to generation. Since then, they have been used by families and organizations in different ways over the years, with the similar purpose of protecting assets so they can continue to grow.

There are a number of different perks to setting up a Family Trust: shielding from taxes, government, or creditors, and keeping control over your assets for the beneficiaries of the trust.

It all sounds very high level, but they are really quite straightforward once you boil it down. The basic setup is like any other investment account, but with a few nuances once you get it going. The main difference between a Trust account and a regular investment account is that a group of people (such as other family members or beneficiaries) are taxed on the income and gains, so the income can be split among the beneficiaries.

For example, the beneficiaries would be your children, minors, or a spouse who are not working or are earning income at a lower income level. Another example would be elderly parents whose retirement you want to help fund or whose retirement income you want to supplement, or whose care you want to pay for. You can really tailor a Family Trust for any specific need you have within your family.

Why is this a particularly effective strategy for a family with some wealth built up and the capacity for larger investments?

In order to make a Family Trust work, you do need a certain amount of capital to get it going. Basically, the minimum threshold would be roughly $500,000. The strategy can work for lower amounts to start, but in order to make the setup cost, and time and effort of managing it worthwhile it does require a certain amount of investible capital. That is not to say that it's a huge amount of time and effort, but be prepared for some additional record keeping and a bit of time to set-up properly. Once a trust is up and running, the ongoing maintenance is fairly straightforward.

How does this actually work?

For us, it really starts with getting to know your family's needs. I will touch on a few examples, but one of the most common ones is that people use it for income to split with their minor-aged children or elderly parents. The government has strict attribution rules that prevent someone from simply gifting money to their children to invest on their behalf. Therefore, you cannot just give money to your children without the taxes floating back up to your tax rate. If you are a high income earner at the top marginal tax rate, there's no point in putting money in your children's hands, as it just ends up being taxed at your full rate.

What a trust allows you to do is to split income among the beneficiaries. The way a trust is generally set-up is that one of the trustees, parents or the trust's settlor loans the money to the trust for the benefit of the beneficiaries. Because the funds are loaned to the trust according to the government's prescribed interest rate on a temporary basis, it is not considered a gift and doesn't trigger income attribution rules.

Who Does It Work For?

When you start setting it up, you want to tailor it specifically for the needs of your family. One of the best examples and most popular ways to make the most out of the Family Trust structure is when a family has minor-aged children. Let us use a family with two young children who participate in a variety of activities such as music lessons, hockey, skiing, dance etc. as an example. These days, children usually have a full schedule of activities and the costs add up in a hurry. They may also go to private school.. These are all examples of a great case where you can pay for things that you are paying for anyway, and do it on a more tax-advantaged basis. As I will explain, this means major opportunities for saving.

The Set-Up Process

The first step is determining who the trustees, the settlor and who the beneficiaries are. In the example above, the trustees would likely be the parents and the beneficiaries would be the children. They may choose to add a third trustee, as one would do when setting up a will, to cover off any unforeseen circumstances. We always work with a lawyer to make sure that everything is structured properly for every situation. It is similar to setting up a holding company, and it is important to use someone qualified to manage the process and document everything properly.

There is always a third party involved in setting up a trust called a settlor. The role of the settlor is to settle the trust by gifting an asset to it. This may sound somewhat archaic, but in most cases the lawyer will have the settlor purchase a unique gold or silver coin that is the settlement property that remains with the trust. There is a lot of history to this tradition that I won't get into in this guidebook, but it is an interesting concept and does formalize the process.

Once the Family Trust is established and the trustees have signed off, the trust is officially registered and then it is ready to go. The next step is funding the trust account and this is done by technically loaning the Trust the money. It is important to structure the loan to the trust properly so that the lenders are not subject to any 'attribution' rules for the income that is generated within the Trust. Attribution rules effectively prevent you from just giving money directly to minor age children to save tax or split income. Normally, the way the government has the tax rules set up, if you're a high income earner, and want to pass along money to your children, anything that they earn on it ends up being taxed at your full marginal tax rate. This rule makes it so that there is no benefit to you, or your children, for splitting the money out that way.

On the other hand, if you put it into a Trust vehicle and you loan the Trust the money then the same attribution rules don't apply. The loan does have to comply with the government's prescribed rate which, in the current low interest rate environment, is at all-time lows of 1% interest per year. The current 1% rate can be locked-in for as long as the loan is in place and the life of the trust.

I will stress this and repeat this: this is a very low rate to set up and lock in for this type of loan, and the rate remains at the low rate for the life of the trust or the term of the loan.

Once the trust is funded, the cash is invested in a variety of dividend paying stocks, bonds and other investment vehicles according to the risk tolerance and income requirements established by the trustees. From the investments made, any dividend, interest income or capital gains will all flow through to the beneficiaries and is taxed in their hands at their tax rates. This is where the big advantage comes in. Any dividends and capital gains retain their character and are taxed at a very low rate in the hands of the beneficiaries. Even regular interest income, which is normally taxed at an individual's top marginal tax rate, can be a highly efficient way to earn income because the beneficiaries are generally taxed at a much lower rate.

Simply put: when your Trust account grows, earns income, or collects dividends, and the funds are allocated out to the beneficiaries, you don't pay tax at your personal tax rate, but rather that of your children or the trust's beneficiaries. It also reduces the income that would normally be taxed in your hands at your top rate.

The chart below illustrates how the flow of funds works from the lender to the trust to the beneficiaries. In this example, $1 million is loaned to the trust at 1%. The trust pays interest on the loan each year of $10,000 and the balance of the income, capital gains and dividends flows to the beneficiaries.

Formal Trust Structure

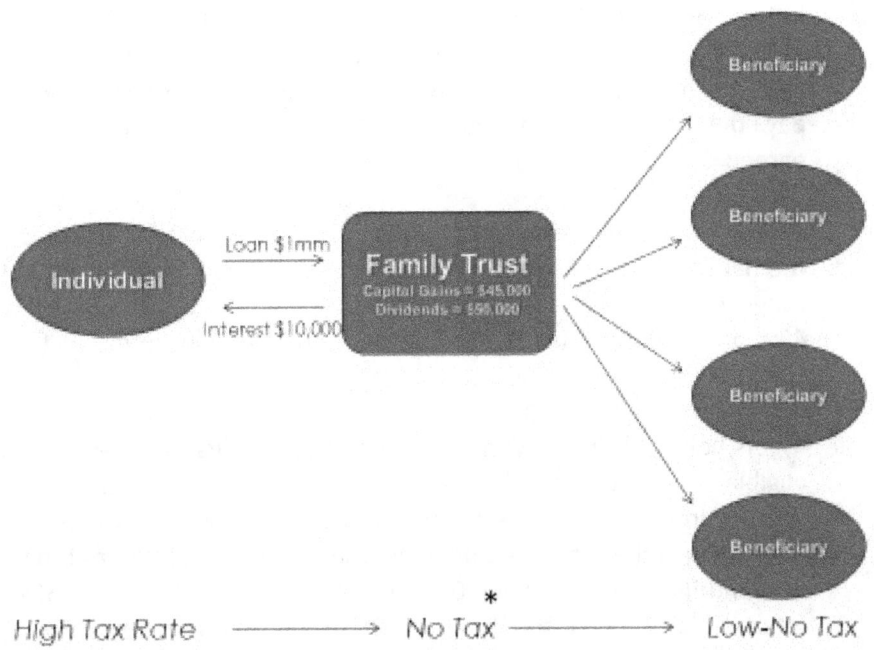

*No tax would be paid by the trust itself assuming that all the income and gains earned in the trust are distributed to the beneficiaries. Otherwise, any earnings retained in the trust would be taxed at the top marginal tax rate.

What is the best way to invest the funds in the trust?

The best investment strategy for the funds in the trust really depends on each individual's own situation and risk tolerance. However, there are some significant advantages to investing the funds in a trust in companies that pay eligible Canadian dividends and allocating the dividends to Canadian beneficiaries.

For example, if your child does not yet have a job or other source of income, they would fall into the lowest tax rate. Across Canada, the basic exemption for 2016 is $11,474, meaning that no tax is paid on the first $11,474 earned either provincially or federally. For a top income earner, like a doctor or lawyer making more than $300,000 per year they would pay now 48% in Alberta and more in other provinces on that same income earned.

Therefore, the tax savings on $11,000 of investment income generated in the hands of a low-income earner vs a high income earner work out to roughly $5,500 per year. (Rounding off for simplicity and using half or 48% of $11,000). This is the first and most basic example of the tax savings that are available.

It gets better though. With the dividend tax credits that are applied to eligible Canadian dividends, the first roughly $40,000 of dividend income comes through nearly **tax-free** to low income earners. It varies slightly depending in the province, but across the country very little tax is paid on dividend income up to $40,000. Comparing this to the nearly 50% tax rates on income at the top income levels and the tax savings are substantial.

The following examples use a tax calculator that is available online at: http://www.tax-services.ca/income-tax-calculator-canada/

If we input a hypothetical situation where an individual in Alberta or Ontario earns $10,000 of income from interest and $30,000 from eligible Canadian dividends the result is a tax bill of only $385 or about 1%.

Ontario Income Tax Calculator | ON

You'll owe about **$385** in taxes: **$385** in federal tax and **$0** in Ontario provincial tax.

Your average tax rate is **1.0%** and your marginal rate is **31.2%**.

Province

| Ontario | ON   ⌄ |

First, you can calculate your income tax combined federal and provincial tax bill in Ontario by entering your annual income.

Annual Income

| $10,000 |

And then you can estimate your tax refund by entering your taxes paid, RRSP contributions and capital gains for the year 2015.

Taxes Paid

| $ |

Please enter your income taxes that are automatically taken out of your paychecks.

RRSPs Made

| $ |

If you've made your RRSP contribution for the year 2015 or 2016, you can enter them here.

Capital Gains

| $ |

Eligible Dividends

| $30,000 |

Please enter other Income such as Investments

Ineligible Dividends

| $ |

Source: http://www.tax-services.ca/on-ontario-income-tax-calculator/

Comparing this to the tax rate on a high-income earner in Ontario who earns, for example $410,000 of income (combined from employment and investments) and $30,000 of dividends the average tax rate is 40.5%.

Ontario Income Tax Calculator | ON

You'll owe about **$178,280** in taxes: **$112,446** in federal tax and **$65,834** in Ontario provincial tax.

Your average tax rate is **40.5%** and your marginal rate is **46.4%**.

Province

Ontario | ON

First, you can calculate your income tax combined federal and provincial tax bill in Ontario by entering your annual income.

Annual Income

$410,000

And then you can estimate your tax refund by entering your taxes paid, RRSP contributions and capital gains for the year 2015.

Taxes Paid

$

Please enter your income taxes that are automatically taken out of your paychecks.

RRSPs Made

$

If you've made your RRSP contribution for the year 2015 or 2016, you can enter them here.

Capital Gains

$

Eligible Dividends

$30,000

Please enter other Income such as Investments

Ineligible Dividends

$

Source: http://www.tax-services.ca/on-ontario-income-tax-calculator/
If this same individual was able to allocate $10,000 of investment income and $30,000 of dividend income to their trust and into the hands of each

beneficiary at their lower tax rate, tax savings work out to over **$13,000 per year.** This can be done across several beneficiaries and the tax savings multiply even further.

(To note: this example simplifies the scenario by ignoring the impact of the interest that would need to be paid on loan from the trustee at 1% - we will incorporate this into a full example later on, but the overall impact is minimal.)

As you can see, this becomes a very effective tool for income splitting. The money that is earned in the trust can then be allocated to each beneficiary or child and used to pay for school or extracurricular activities. For example, private school, sports, music or nearly any extracurricular activity can be paid for using the money from the Trust account that was taxed at a much lower rate.

This can work out to savings of over 40% on activities and children's expenses that you are paying for anyway. If you are already starting to do the math in your head, you can see how this adds up to major savings over the span of time you are raising your children.

The prior examples use Ontario as a tax jurisdiction, but the tax savings are about the same in Alberta starting in 2016. Below is a table that compares the tax rates in Alberta from 2015 to 2016. As you can see, the top level for earned income is now 48% tax on any income earned over $300,000, up from 40.25% in 2015.

Alberta (AB) Personal Income Tax Brackets and Tax Rates

2016 Taxable Income	2016 Tax Rates	2015 Taxable Income	2015 Tax Rates
first $125,000	10%	first $125,000	10.00%
over $125,000 up to $150,000	12%	over $125,000 up to $150,000	10.50%
over $150,000 up to $200,000	13%	over $150,000 up to $200,000	10.75%
over $200,000 up to $300,000	14%	over $200,000 up to $300,000	11.00%
over $300,000	15%	over $300,000	11.25%

Combined Federal & Alberta Tax Brackets and Tax Rates

2016 Taxable Income	2016 Marginal Tax Rates				2015 Taxable Income	2015 Marginal Tax Rates			
	Other Income	Capital Gains	Canadian Dividends			Other Income	Capital Gains	Canadian Dividends	
			Eligible	Non-Eligible				Eligible	Non-Eligible
first $45,282	25.0%	12.50%	-0.03%	13.33%	first $44,701	25.00%	12.50%	-0.03%	12.84%
over $45,282 up to $90,563	30.5%	15.25%	7.56%	19.77%	over $44,701 up to $89,401	32.00%	16.00%	9.63%	21.10%
over $90,563 up to $125,000	36.0%	18.00%	15.15%	26.20%	over $89,401 up to $125,000	36.00%	18.00%	15.15%	25.82%
over $125,000 up to $140,388	38.0%	19.00%	17.91%	28.54%	over $125,000 up to $136,586	36.50%	18.25%	15.84%	26.41%
over $140,388 up to $150,000	41.0%	20.50%	22.05%	32.05%	over $138,586 up to $150,000	39.50%	19.75%	19.98%	29.95%
over $150,000 up to $200,000	42.0%	21.00%	23.43%	33.22%	over $150,000 up to $200,000	39.75%	19.88%	20.33%	30.25%
over $200,000 up to $300,000	47.0%	23.50%	30.33%	39.07%	over $200,000 up to $300,000	40.00%	20.00%	20.67%	30.54%
over $300,000	48.0%	24.00%	31.71%	40.24%	over $300,000	40.25%	20.13%	21.02%	30.84%

Marginal tax rate for dividends is a % of actual dividends received (not grossed-up amount).
Marginal tax rate for capital gains is a % of total capital gains (not taxable capital gains).
Gross-up rate for eligible dividends is 38%, and for non-eligible dividends is 17% in 2016, 18% in 2015.
2016 non-eligible dividend rates reflect the dividend tax credit rate as per Alberta's October 2015 Bill 4.
For more information see Alberta dividend tax credits.

Source: http://www.taxtips.ca/taxrates/ab.htm

Is this similar to running a holding company and keeping track of investments and expenses?

Yes, it is similar to that. In this case you're making the most of the government's graduated tax system.

In Alberta, the new NDP government has announced much higher taxes on high-income earners. As opposed to the flat 10% provincial tax that Albertans used to enjoy, higher income earners will now be taxed at a top marginal rate of 15% on every dollar earned over $300,000 per year at the provincial level.

At the Federal level the tax rates ramp up quite quickly as well. The top tax rate at the Federal level starts at $200,000. Therefore, high income Albertans will now be taxed at a combined federal and provincial rate of 48% on their income over $300,000, as opposed 39% that was charged in the past. However, someone on the lower end of the tax scale, making for example, $25,000 per year would still pay very little in tax. The Family Trust would allow you to split some of the money made at the top end of someone's income down to someone in the lower tax brackets.

These are very significant tax savings, especially when you add up all the benefits of spreading that income across numerous individuals in lower tax brackets. Efficient income splitting is a significant advantage of using a Family Trust.

I should mention that it doesn't apply just to children. It can be a spouse who is not working, or who is working part time, or an elderly parent or family member you want to help take care of. It can be tailored to almost any type of family situation.

So by paying for things like lessons or private school fees through the Trust, you are using funds that are taxed at a much lower rate. You are effectively paying 35-45% less than those who are not using a Family Trust.

To take the example further, if you add up a child's expenses throughout the year, whether it's private school, or hockey, or music lessons, and it comes to $15,000, the savings can be roughly $7000, depending on the specific tax brackets and situation. That savings adds up for **each** child, every single year, compared to keeping the income in your own name and paying your full tax rate. This adds up significantly over time.

In Canada, the tax rule is that, as a parent, you need to provide food, clothing, and shelter for your children. You cannot pay for those things out of Family Trust, but all the extracurricular activities and items or expenses like private school are eligible. Anything that is above and beyond the basic necessities of life can be considered additional 'expenses' for your children or beneficiaries. Depending on your situation, this can also include childcare, or a full-time nanny. The same structure can be used to pay for the needs or expenses related to the care of elderly parents or relatives. It is quite versatile, and fits many different lifestyles and family configurations. As a result, it is an incredibly effective tax saving tool.

It is No Surprise That Having Children is Expensive...

Especially if you are looking at the best schools, or they start to have success in sports or music where they move to more advanced levels. Schools in Calgary, just for kindergarten, can be over $10,000 a year. It goes up and up, as you get into higher levels. The going rate for any private school in the country can be pretty high, and isn't likely to go down over time.

Can the Family Trust system apply to University costs as well, or does it cut off once the children are not minors?

Yes, you can use it for expenses such as University as well. However, there are other programs that you can take advantage of, such as the RESP or Registered Education Savings Plan programs, that we advise all clients with families about. The RESP program includes some government grants and a tax-sheltered structure that will allow you to grow your savings for a child's education. We can take a look at anyone's personal situation and determine which structure fits the best for paying for a university education. The nice thing about a Family Trust is that there are really no age restrictions on who the beneficiaries are. The income splitting works just as well if the individual beneficiary is over 18, but still in a low tax bracket.

Why Does the Trust concept fit so well with our investment strategies?

To make the most of the Family Trust portfolio, we use a variety of investment instruments that are personalized for each individual's situation. The advantage that we have in working with an independent advisory team is that we take the time to really learn what the trust will be used for and how best to take advantage of the structure to maximize the benefit in the lowest risk way.

Obviously, we're looking for investments that go up in value. That is the most basic concept of investing. Capital gains are always important, but most often the goal of a Family Trust is to generate ongoing income for the beneficiaries. Capital gains are included at half the tax rate of regular income and are one of the most tax efficient ways to capture gains. However, due to the nature of market fluctuations, it can be difficult to get the timing of capital gains to match with the income needs of the beneficiaries, as capital gains are dependent on when you buy and sell.

When we focus on income, you will see in the table below that the government has a very favorable treatment for eligible Canadian dividends, especially at the lower tax rates. (The appendix of this book has tables that show the tax rates for each province and territory for income, dividends, and capital gains.) Each province has its own table of tax rates for different types of investments.

If you are in a roughly $40,000 or lower tax bracket, as your beneficiaries will likely be, you'll see that eligible Canadian dividends are nearly tax-free in almost every Canadian Province. The exceptions being Manitoba and Quebec, where they're taxed at a rate between 6%-11% (still a very low rate and a fraction of what they would be taxed in the hands of a high income earner). For almost every other Province and Territory, income from eligible Canadian dividends is tax free, up to the first $40,000 per person in a given year.

Every investor does have their own risk tolerance with investing. In order to get dividends, you have to invest in the common stocks or equity of a company which are subject to the volatility of the public markets. If you're a lower risk investor, Family Trust can still be very effective. If you prefer fixed income investments, the strategy still works quite well, but the tax rates just aren't quite as good when compared to earning income through dividends as a Canadian. At lower income levels, the first $11,000 of income earned in a given year, is also tax-free in nearly every province. Even getting up to $20,000 to $30,000 per year of income, the average tax rates are still much lower than what someone earning $300,000 would be taxed.

A fixed income allocation in an investment portfolio can have the effect of stabilizing the investment portfolio and to reducing volatility generally. Unfortunately, the drawback is that the income generated is taxed more heavily than the income from the dividends of Canadian companies. When structuring the investments in the Trust account we will get to know every client and their goals and risk tolerances in order to optimize the investment strategy.

How do we balance different investment types for maximum benefit?

We're always somewhat active on accounts. Any time there is a large gain that can be had on a specific stock, we often look to trade some of that positon or sell all or part of it just to reduce our exposure, and perhaps look for an opportunity to buy back in if things look like they have run too far, too quickly. There are a number of strategies we use to take advantage of each type of investment, depending on whether we are looking for capital gains, income, or dividends. Generally, we strive for a blend. We always look to tailor a strategy specifically for each client's needs.

We recommend multi-generation thinking, but how long do these Trust accounts run for? How do they get passed on?

The Trust has an interesting structure. The laws of Canada dictate that the assets in an inter-vivos Trust are subject to a deemed disposition every 21 years. After this point the taxes must be paid on any capital gains and the trust can continue or be wound up if there is no longer a need for it. Most people will find that a 21-year life is a sufficient span of time to make the most out of the setup.

The reason we strongly recommend it to families with children, is that the specific needs generally fall within that 21-year journey of raising children and paying for their schooling, extracurricurals and getting them started in life. It provides a system that works from birth through to early adulthood and into university years, depending on when you start it. If you start it a bit later, you can use it to help them out with some extra income through their early 20s if you choose to. Once the beneficiaries are established in life and they are through University, college or have a stable job earning their own income, the trust can be closed down. At this point you can simply wind it up and the original loan is paid back to the original lender and the trust ceases to exist. If you still have a situation where you would see the benefits of a trust, you would have to setup a new Family Trust, with a new set of goals.

Are there any other uses for a Family Trust?

There are other uses for a Trust in financial planning. Families can use them for things like holding a cabin or cottage that has been in the family, for managing the costs and passing it through generations. In other applications a Trust can be used to share and pass along investment in family businesses, farms, or real estate, and so on. However, special consideration needs to be made when dealing with real estate or other illiquid assets to ensure that the 21-year deemed disposition rule doesn't cause tax problems at the end of the 21-year timeframe. This type of structure is possible but it is outside the scope of this book.

Once you understand how it works, you see that there are many situations that are best served through the use of a trust. The Family Trust is sometimes described as being almost like a Swiss army knife of investment tools. You can have your screw driver, your knife, the little saw etc.

With the Trust setup, there are a multitude of different applications, and we're here to tailor it specifically to your needs. We have the process to get it set up and running so that you get the maximum benefit, and you continually build wealth and keep in in your family.

So I lend the Trust a lump sum to get it started. Do I get this back?

It is important to structure the trust properly and use professionals to help make sure that it is following all of the government rules. One of the primary requirements when you lend funds to the trust you must make the loan at the government's prescribed interest rate. The government sets the minimum prescribed interest rate and revises it quarterly based on a pre-determined formula. This is the minimum rate at which you are allowed to loan money. In the current low interest rate environment, the prescribed rate is 1% per year. This is the lowest it has ever been and there is really no way for it to get any lower. The next stop is zero, and it is very unlikely that the government will ever drop it to that level. Basically, if you start right now, the Trust borrows this money at 1% and this loan rate is set for the life of the trust or up to 21 years. The trust has to pay the lender for the 1% interest on the total amount of the loan every year. Then any income in the trust, above that 1% level would fall to the beneficiaries.

Let's go back to our example of a family with two children. The parents set-up a trust with an initial loan of $1 million and in a given year the trust earns the earns $40,000 dividends, $30,000 worth of capital gains and $20,000 in interest income net of management expenses. The dividends, capital gains and income would flow down and be split by the beneficiaries, minus the 1% interest paid out on the loan. In this case the loan interest works out to $10,000, that would be paid out to the initial lender who set up the trust and offset against the income that was earned.

	Gross	Net	Per Child
Dividend income	$30,000	$30,000	$15,000
Capital gains	$30,000	$30,000	$15,000
Interest income	$20,000	$10,000	$5,000
Loan interest paid	-$10,000		
Total	$70,000	$70,000	$35,000

The result is that each child would receive $35,000 of income that is taxed in their hands to be allocated against eligible expenses. Plugging these numbers into the online tax calculator shows that the tax paid for an Alberta, BC or Ontario resident is only $215 or less than 1%. If you were to add these amounts on top the income of a high-income earner, the tax paid is $35-45% depending on the province.

Do I have to keep adding to it? Is this recommended? Or do I just set it up and let it grow?

You have the option to add to it, if it makes sense or if you have additional income needs for the beneficiaries over time. If you have the means to fully fund a trust on day one, it makes sense to do so and take advantage of the low 1% prescribed rate. It can make sense to add to a trust as your savings grow and the beneficiaries have greater needs. If you do add to a trust over time with subsequent loans, they will have to be at the prescribed rate of the day.

It doesn't make sense to over-fund a Trust. It is possible that it becomes so successful that you get to the point where your beneficiaries are getting into their maximum tax rates or you don't have enough eligible expenses to allocate all trust income out. Once you hit this point, you're starting lose the benefits of the Trust structure. If you get to that point, it likely makes more sense just to keep that money in your own personal accounts and keep it invested in your own name.

There's a sweet spot for how much you put in, depending on how many beneficiaries you have, and what their needs are. You can also adapt a trust as things change, for example, if a family member needed at-home care, you can put more funds in the trust by way of a new loan and use it to pay for this new need and keep the benefits going longer.

What does it take to get a Family Trust started? What is the process?

The first thing we do is get to know your situation. That is what we do with every potential client that applies to work with us. We are talking about a plan that will have us working together for decades, so it is really important to us that it is the right fit. We need to make sure that this type of structure makes sense for you, and that our strategies fit with your goals.

Assessing whether you have the capital to invest to make this structure worthwhile is the first step, either as a lump-sum investment, or a commitment to annual contributions.

We also talk about your beneficiaries and their needs. We want to make sure you are in a position to be able to take advantage of the income splitting aspect. Do you have multiple dependents at lower tax brackets? For example, children or a lower income spouse? If you have sufficient investment capital and you have members of your family with various expenses throughout the year, then this type of strategy would most likely make sense for you.

Once we determine that the Family Trust setup is right for you and that we will work well together, we get the setup process started. It takes a team of people to make sure it is done properly. We work with specialized law firms and accountants to make sure everything is done correctly, and that you are properly educated to make the most of the benefits of this structure.

The Family Trust is similar to a holding company, so the trust itself files its own tax returns. As a result, the beneficiaries will also need to file their own tax returns. This creates an added layer of complexity and some costs every tax year, but it's not overly daunting. It is quite routine once you understand the process and work with the right professionals.

So there is an educational component? It sounds like some extra work...

If this is the first you have heard of it, it might sound a little bit scary having to file a number of extra tax returns and adding extra accounting work at tax time. It is quite straightforward once you have a system in place. The investments are easy to track and are summarized at year-end.

In order to offset any expenses in the hands of the beneficiaries you will need to keep track of your receipts from any activities that you want to include. For example, most people would want to offset the expenses for private school, sports, music and any related travel for these programs. It is as simple as tracking the expenses throughout the year, and paying the bills as they come in. It doesn't take a great deal of time each month to manage this as there are generally only a half dozen items to track in a given month. The trust has its own cheque book or transfer system, and cheques are written or funds are transferred from the trust's bank account to pay for expenses directly. . Once you setup the trust and have it running, you get a direct sense of the savings on a regular basis. After a couple of months, you definitely see that it's a worthwhile exercise.

What are the costs to get this started?

There is a setup fee that for starting a trust that is similar to incorporating a small business or holding company. To setup a simple trust that covers most families needs usually costs a few thousand dollars, but the cost can be higher depending on the complexity and the law firm that is used. We work with law firms that do this on a regular basis and can setup a simple trust quite efficiently. The setup of the trust is an important step as it is key to get the trust structured properly at the outset to make sure that it works for your family's particular situation and needs. While the trust is being setup, we will also be meeting with you so that we get to know more about your goals for your investments. For most people the cost is easily justified, even in the first year when considering the tax savings.

It becomes more complicated if you have, for example, real estate or a farm or some other issues in your business or other things you want to protect with the trust structure. In these cases we need to run through all the details with all parties involved, to come up with an exact cost.

Once your Trust is up and running, there are some annual expenses and administration costs. These will include the bookkeeping and accounting to organize and file the taxes for the Trust, and the individual taxes for the beneficiaries involved. The great thing is that all of these costs can be written off as expenses against the income of the Trust itself. We mentioned the benefits of paying these expenses with pre-tax dollars adding up to 30-40% savings. As a result, the expenses are a relatively small part of the overall cost savings that the trust enables.

My Family Trust Experience

I've had a Family Trust set up for a couple of years now. I have three children in private school and they're in different sports, music lessons, and after school programs. It has made a huge change in terms of how we, as a family, approach and understand our finances.

Nobody likes getting bills. The costs of school and activities are often enough to make you wince when you open that mail. But I have to admit, it's a great feeling paying these expenses directly from the trust and knowing that I'm getting what amounts to up to a 48% discount on all of these bills. The savings add up quickly.

It also gives me the confidence that it all fits in as part of the plan. It is nice knowing that I have this extra account that I have already budgeted for, and have allocated funds for this situation. There are no surprises. There is never any scrambling or juggling to find the funds. It is taken care of. You have dividends coming every month or quarter, to cover all offsets. It is an incredibly satisfying exercise to work through, knowing that you have a great structure that is taking care of itself, and helping look after the family.

From my experience, it's something I would highly recommend to people with children in any kinds of activities, or to people who have family members that need any kind of care. I know that I'm just at the beginning of getting the benefit of my Family Trust. My children are still young and nothing they are doing is getting any cheaper. School gets costlier as they get into higher grades. Field trips take them further away. I hear from friends that their children's hockey teams going down to the US or even to Europe for tournaments in later years. In addition, of course, there is university or college and the list goes on. I want to be able to provide great opportunities for my children to have a solid upbringing and be able to pay for it all. The Family Trust setup gives me confidence that I will be able to fulfill this goal.

How much time does it take to organize all of this on an ongoing basis?

Part of our program is that we set you up with an efficient system, so that it's as quick and easy as possible for you to make this part of your monthly routine. We set you up with the education, systems and pre-designed spreadsheets so that it's simple to track expenses every month.

Come tax time, there will be a meeting with the bookkeeper who goes through everything with you and makes sure it's all ready for tax filing. When people are organized and have used the system properly, they find it takes less than a half hour per month, just to tally up the monthly receipts, and input the data into the spreadsheet, and write the appropriate cheques. Once people get into the groove with the right system, it's not a particularly onerous process. It's very clean and straightforward.

And for $2000, or $5000, or $20,000 worth of savings, as well as the peace of mind it brings, this time spent is highly worth it. As you work through it, it doesn't feel like a chore, because you're paying yourself with the dividends and income, and covering off a number of expenses that otherwise would have come right out of your pocket.

The great thing is that it doesn't require any mastery of special software, or advanced knowledge of accounting. We make sure to set it all up so it's as clean and easy for you as possible. We want you to spend your time doing the more important things, while still getting the maximum benefit from your hard earned money.

So in total what does this cost? Are there ongoing costs associated with managing this program?

The Trust itself has an annual filing which the lawyers who set it up will handle. Law firms usually charge a couple of hundred dollars a year for the maintenance of the minute books and the Trust records. That particular cost is paid for by the funds in the Trust. There is the cost to prepare the tax filings such as bookkeeping and tax preparation. There is also the cost of managing the investments themselves, but any investment management fees would also be paid by the trust on an ongoing basis.

What are the costs of managing the investments in the Trust account?

This is definitely an important consideration. The accounting and legal fees are straightforward. Part of our offering is that we take the time to personalize the investments in the trust to suit every client's particular needs and risk tolerances. We charge a flat investment management fee that is paid directly from the trust and is deductible against taxes paid. Our rates are very competitive with other offerings in the market. The cost of management is taken care of by the dividends that come into the trust account, so you aren't writing a cheque out of pocket each month.

We actively manage and track all of the investments in our client's trust and investment accounts. We are always watching out for opportunities to take capital gains and monitoring companies' financial strength and sustainability of their dividends. This is our main area of expertise and our clients get very good value and our returns have been very strong historically.

We always recommend that clients allow us to manage investments in the account on a day-to-day basis, while keeping them up to date on the progress on a monthly or quarterly basis. This approach tends to work the best as most clients have busy lives and don't need to be involved in the nuance of every investment decision. Because we know each client's goals and have an idea of their monthly cash needs when we start out, we work to make sure that there are always funds available when needed.

You can put whatever investments in a Family Trust that you choose. However, in our world, the goal is to build a solid portfolio of dividend paying companies and high quality fixed income investments. We look for sustainable dividends and generally companies with low debt levels. The investment approach to a Family Trust is thinking long-term. This is a plan that is set up for decades and generations, and it is not generally home to the volatile penny-stocks or start-ups. This is where your more stable capital is and this is how we help you build wealth for the long run. It is not always flashy. But it works.

It is important to understand that our costs, the actual cost for managing the account, are a fixed cost tied to the total that's in the account. This is opposed to the traditional stockbroker commission fee set-up. We aren't charging a fee every time we make a transaction. It is not about constantly buying and selling. The more the account grows, the better both parties do. This setup is the best alignment of incentives between the client and the advisor team. As an investor, it is comforting to know that your account manager shares the same motivation as you: your success.

Can the Trust be used to educate the children about money and personal finances?

It is not specifically designed as such, but it really depends on each family's philosophy and how they want to handle this issue. We certainly encourage getting the children involved, when the time is right. The main benefit of the Trust, in this regard, is that it makes it an easy and clear conversation to have with your children. On some level, they see you making intelligent financial decisions, and you can teach them the same concepts.

For many wealthy families, this question is a kind of elephant in the room, so to speak. As a well-off family, how do you teach your children about money, and how do you bring them into that conversation? Nearly every parent wants the best for their children and the ability to experience the best opportunities in life. While at the same time, there is a balance between having advantages and spoiling them or giving them a sense of entitlement. It is a tricky balance. I have heard from many families that the Trust lays a nice framework to start this education.

The other thing is that, as the children grow into adulthood, the assets in the Trust account can smoothly transition into something like a family foundation that you run, and have your children help select what charitable causes you want to support, and really use it as something to keep the family close and to create a bond. There are many different ways that the trust structure, and others that are similar, can help families talk about money, manage budgets, and plan generationally.

How to speak with your family about money and finances definitely depends on each individual's personal philosophy. However, it is often the case that open discussions around how to manage finances and investments is something that is often ignored or simply not raised during childhood. The trust setup can help bring that conversation into the forefront, as opposed to just sweeping it under the carpet. It makes intelligent management a part of life, rather than something that can become scary, ignored, or a burden thanks to not growing up with the proper financial education.

One of the nice things about the philosophy of the trust is that it is a very thoughtful approach. It is not flashy or aggressive. The whole idea is to set up a structure that provides security and stability to your family's financial affairs. It does take some time and energy to put in place but the benefits are significant in the long term.

In Summary

These trusts can be customized for most family situations. It is currently one of the best tools available to grow your wealth and reduce your tax burden. If you have some investment capital and have beneficiaries be it children, spouse, elderly parents, cousins, someone with special needs, setting up a Family Trust will most likely make a lot of sense.

Once you qualify, we can start the process and tailor your Family Trust to your unique needs and goals.

Why start now?

This point bears repeating. Interest rates right now are hovering around 1%. It can't get much lower, and can only go up. It has fluctuated quite a bit over the years, and the government does review it on a regular basis. When the economy eventually picks up, it is likely that the government will eventually raise the prescribed interest rate to 2% or higher. At this point the Family Trust structure can still work, but it is not as efficient as it is using a loan at a 1% rate.

There is a certain impetus to get started now, because the rate you start at is locked-in for the life of the loan and therefore the life of the trust. If the initial loan to fund the trust is at 1%, that is where it stays for the next 21 years or until you wind up the trust or repay the loan. And the lower the interest rates, the better this system works!

The other reason to start now is that the tax savings start in the first year that you set it up and go on for the life of the trust. Taxes just went up significantly for high-income earners in Alberta and across the country, making a Family Trust an even better tool for tax planning.

How do I qualify to work with you and your team?

If you are interested in pursuing this strategy or have any questions please give us a call. We are available to discuss in more detail and help you set-up and implement this strategy for your family.

www.mackiewealthgroup.com

2016 Provincial tax rates for Income, Capital Gains, Non-Eligible dividends and Eligible Dividends

British Columbia 2016

Marginal Tax Rates (%)

Taxable Income ($)	Interest and Regular Income	Capital Gains	Non-eligible Canadian Dividends	Eligible Canadian Dividends
0 to 11,474	-	-	-	-
11,474 to 19,000	15.00	7.50	4.70	-0.03
19,000 to 32,100	23.56	11.78	11.74	-2.02
32,100 to 38,210	20.06	10.03	8.27	-6.85
38,210 to 45,282	22.70	11.35	11.36	-3.20
45,282 to 76,421	28.20	14.10	17.79	4.39
76,421 to 87,741	31.00	15.50	21.07	8.25
87,741 to 90,563	32.79	16.40	23.16	10.72
90,563 to 106,543	38.29	19.15	29.60	18.31
106,543 to 140,388	40.70	20.35	32.42	21.64
140,388 to 200,000	43.70	21.85	35.93	25.78
200,000 and over	47.70	23.85	40.61	31.30

Alberta 2016

Marginal Tax Rates (%)

Taxable Income ($)	Interest and Regular Income	Capital Gains	Non-eligible Canadian Dividends	Eligible Canadian Dividends
0 to 11,474	-	-	-	-
11,474 to 18,214	15.00	7.50	4.70	-0.03
18,214 to 45,282	25.00	12.50	13.33	-0.03
45,282 to 90,563	30.50	15.25	19.77	7.56
90,563 to 125,000	36.00	18.00	26.20	15.15
125,000 to 140,388	38.00	19.00	28.54	17.91
140,388 to 150,000	41.00	20.50	32.05	22.05
150,000 to 200,000	42.00	21.00	33.22	23.43
200,000 to 300,000	47.00	23.50	39.07	30.33
300,000 and over	48.00	24.00	40.24	31.71

Saskatchewan 2016

Marginal Tax Rates (%)

Taxable Income ($)	Interest and Regular Income	Capital Gains	Non-eligible Canadian Dividends	Eligible Canadian Dividends
0 to 11,474	-	-	-	-
11,474 to 15,639	15.00	7.50	4.70	-0.03
15,639 to 44,601	26.00	13.00	14.32	-0.03
44,601 to 45,282	28.00	14.00	16.66	2.73
45,282 to 90,563	33.50	16.75	23.10	10.32
90,563 to 127,430	39.00	19.50	29.53	17.91
127,430 to 140,388	41.00	20.50	31.87	20.67
140,388 to 200,000	44.00	22.00	35.38	24.81
200,000 and over	48.00	24.00	40.06	30.33

Manitoba 2016

Marginal Tax Rates (%)

Taxable Income ($)	Interest and Regular Income	Capital Gains	Non-eligible Canadian Dividends	Eligible Canadian Dividends
0 to 11,474	-	-	-	-
11,474 to 15,411	15.00	7.50	4.70	-0.03
15,411 to 22,944	34.80	17.40	27.08	16.25
22,944 to 31,000	25.80	12.90	16.90	3.83
31,000 to 45,282	27.75	13.88	19.19	6.53
45,282 to 67,000	33.25	16.63	25.62	14.12
67,000 to 90,563	37.90	18.95	31.06	20.53
90,563 to 140,388	43.40	21.70	37.50	28.12
140,388 to 200,000	46.40	23.20	41.01	32.26
200,000 and over	50.40	25.20	45.69	37.78

Ontario 2016

Marginal Tax Rates (%)

Taxable Income ($)	Interest and Regular Income	Capital Gains	Non-eligible Canadian Dividends	Eligible Canadian Dividends
0 to 11,474	-	-	-	-
11,474 to 14,376	15.00	7.50	4.70	-0.03
14,376 to 18,891	25.10	12.55	6.00	-13.69
18,891 to 41,536	20.05	10.02	6.13	-6.86
41,536 to 45,282	24.15	12.08	10.93	-1.20
45,282 to 73,145	29.65	14.83	17.37	6.39
73,145 to 83,075	31.48	15.74	19.51	8.92
83,075 to 86,176	33.89	16.95	22.33	12.24
86,176 to 90,563	37.91	18.96	27.03	17.79
90,563 to 140,388	43.41	21.71	33.46	25.37
140,388 to 150,000	46.41	23.21	36.97	29.51
150,000 to 200,000	47.97	23.99	38.80	31.67
200,000 to 220,000	51.97	25.99	43.48	37.19
220,000 and over	53.53	26.77	49.30	39.34

Quebec 2016

Marginal Tax Rates (%)

Taxable Income ($)	Interest and Regular Income	Capital Gains	Non-eligible Canadian Dividends	Eligible Canadian Dividends
0 to 11,474	-	-	-	-
11,474 to 14,280	12.53	6.27	3.93	-0.02
14,280 to 42,390	28.53	14.27	14.85	5.64
42,390 to 45,282	32.53	16.27	19.53	11.16
45,282 to 84,780	37.12	18.56	24.90	17.49
84,780 to 90,563	41.12	20.56	29.58	23.01
90,563 to 103,150	45.71	22.86	34.95	29.35
103,150 to 140,388	47.46	23.73	37.00	31.77
140,388 to 200,000	49.97	24.99	39.93	35.23
200,000 and over	53.31	26.66	43.84	39.83

New Brunswick 2016

Marginal Tax Rates (%)

Taxable Income ($)	Interest and Regular Income	Capital Gains	Non-eligible Canadian Dividends	Eligible Canadian Dividends
0 to 11,474	-	-	-	-
11,474 to 16,077	15.00	7.50	4.70	-0.03
16,077 to 36,875	27.68	13.84	14.94	0.91
36,875 to 40,492	24.68	12.34	11.89	-3.23
40,492 to 45,282	29.82	14.91	17.90	3.86
45,282 to 80,985	35.32	17.66	24.33	11.45
80,985 to 90,563	37.02	18.51	26.32	13.80
90,563 to 131,664	42.52	21.26	32.76	21.39
131,664 to 140,388	43.84	21.92	34.30	23.21
140,388 to 150,000	46.84	23.42	37.81	27.35
150,000 to 200,000	50.00	25.00	41.51	31.71
200,000 to 250,000	54.00	27.00	46.19	37.23
250,000 and over	58.75	29.38	51.75	43.79

Nova Scotia 2016

Marginal Tax Rates (%)

Taxable Income ($)	Interest and Regular Income	Capital Gains	Non-eligible Canadian Dividends	Eligible Canadian Dividends
0 to 11,474	-	-	-	-
11,474 to 11,893	15.00	7.50	4.70	-0.03
11,893 to 15,000	23.79	11.90	10.94	-0.11
15,000 to 21,000	28.79	14.40	16.84	6.79
21,000 to 29,590	23.79	11.90	11.43	-0.11
29,590 to 45,282	29.95	14.98	18.64	8.39
45,282 to 59,180	35.45	17.73	25.07	15.98
59,180 to 90,563	37.17	18.59	27.08	18.35
90,563 to 93,000	42.67	21.33	33.52	25.94
93,000 to 140,388	43.50	21.75	34.49	27.09
140,388 to 150,000	46.50	23.25	38.00	31.23
150,000 to 200,000	50.00	25.00	42.09	36.06
200,000 and over	54.00	27.00	46.77	41.58

PEI 2016

Marginal Tax Rates (%)

Taxable Income ($)	Interest and Regular Income	Capital Gains	Non-eligible Canadian Dividends	Eligible Canadian Dividends
0 to 10,259	-	-	-	-
10,259 to 11,474	9.80	4.90	7.78	-0.97
11,474 to 16,999	24.80	12.40	12.48	-1.00
16,999 to 21,999	29.80	14.90	18.38	5.90
21,999 to 31,984	24.80	12.40	13.14	-1.00
31,984 to 45,282	28.80	14.40	17.82	4.52
45,282 to 63,969	34.30	17.15	24.25	12.12
63,969 to 90,563	37.20	18.60	27.64	16.12
90,563 to 98,145	42.70	21.35	34.08	23.71
98,145 to 140,388	44.37	22.19	35.68	24.57
140,388 to 200,000	47.37	23.69	37.59	28.71
200,000 and over	51.37	25.69	43.87	34.22

Newfoundland & Labrador 2016

Taxable Income ($)	Marginal Tax Rates (%)			
	Interest and Regular Income	Capital Gains	Non-eligible Canadian Dividends	Eligible Canadian Dividends
0 to 11,474	-	-	-	-
11,474 to 18,955	15.00	7.50	4.70	-0.03
18,955 to 23,853	38.70	19.35	27.83	25.23
23,853 to 35,148	22.70	11.35	9.45	3.15
35,148 to 45,282	27.50	13.75	15.07	9.77
45,282 to 70,295	33.00	16.50	21.50	17.36
70,295 to 90,563	33.80	16.90	22.44	18.46
90,563 to 125,500	39.30	19.65	28.87	26.05
125,500 to 140,388	40.30	20.15	30.04	27.43
140,388 to 175,700	43.30	21.65	33.55	31.57
175,700 to 200,000	44.30	22.15	34.72	32.95
200,000 and over	48.30	24.15	39.40	38.47

Northwest Territories 2016

Marginal Tax Rates (%)

Taxable Income ($)	Interest and Regular Income	Capital Gains	Non-eligible Canadian Dividends	Eligible Canadian Dividends
0 to 11,474	-	-	-	-
11,474 to 13,900	15.00	7.50	4.70	-0.03
13,900 to 41,011	20.90	10.45	5.12	-7.76
41,011 to 45,282	23.60	11.80	8.28	-4.03
45,282 to 82,024	29.10	14.55	14.72	3.56
82,024 to 90,563	32.70	16.35	18.93	8.53
90,563 to 133,353	38.20	19.10	25.36	16.12
133,353 to 140,388	40.05	20.03	27.53	18.67
140,388 to 200,000	43.05	21.53	31.04	22.81
200,000 and over	47.05	23.53	35.72	28.33

Nunavut 2016

Marginal Tax Rates (%)

Taxable Income ($)	Interest and Regular Income	Capital Gains	Non-eligible Canadian Dividends	Eligible Canadian Dividends
0 to 11,474	-	-	-	-
11,474 to 12,781	15.00	7.50	4.70	-0.03
12,781 to 43,176	19.00	9.50	6.53	-2.11
43,176 to 45,282	22.00	11.00	10.04	2.03
45,282 to 86,351	27.50	13.75	16.47	9.62
86,351 to 90,563	29.50	14.75	18.81	12.38
90,563 to 140,388	35.00	17.50	25.25	19.97
140,388 to 200,000	40.50	20.25	31.68	27.56
200,000 and over	44.50	22.25	36.36	33.08

Yukon 2016

Marginal Tax Rates (%)

Taxable Income ($)	Interest and Regular Income	Capital Gains	Non-eligible Canadian Dividends	Eligible Canadian Dividends
0 to 11,474	-	-	-	-
11,474 to 16,378	16.28	8.14	5.46	-2.40
16,378 to 24,999	24.40	12.20	12.05	-7.76
24,999 to 45,282	21.40	10.70	9.05	-11.90
45,282 to 90,563	29.50	14.75	18.53	-0.72
90,563 to 140,388	36.90	18.45	27.19	9.49
140,388 to 200,000	41.80	20.90	32.92	16.25
200,000 to 500,000	45.80	22.90	37.60	21.78
500,000 and over	48.00	24.00	40.17	24.81

www.ingramcontent.com/pod-product-compliance
Lightning Source LLC
Chambersburg PA
CBHW070413190526
45169CB00003B/1245